FRANCIS FRITH'S

WEST WILTSHIRE TOWNS

DEE LA VARDERA has lived and worked in Wiltshire since 1971.
A former Head of English, she has regularly written for the
Education Guardian, The Lady, Wiltshire Life and *Farmers Weekly*.
This is her third book for Francis Frith.

FRANCIS FRITH'S
PHOTOGRAPHIC MEMORIES

WEST WILTSHIRE TOWNS

PHOTOGRAPHIC MEMORIES

DEE LA VARDERA

First published in the United Kingdom in 2003 by
Frith Book Company Ltd

Paperback Edition 2003
ISBN 1-85937-680-0

British Library Cataloguing in Publication Data

Francis Frith's West Wiltshire Towns
Dee La Vardera

Frith Book Company Ltd
Frith's Barn, Teffont,
Salisbury, Wiltshire SP3 5QP
Tel: +44 (0) 1722 716 376
Email: info@francisfrith.co.uk
www.francisfrith.co.uk

Printed and bound in Great Britain by MPG Books Ltd, Bodmin, Cornwall

Front Cover: **TROWBRIDGE** *Silver Street 1900* 45344

Frontispiece: **BRADFORD-ON-AVON,** *The View from Winsley Road c1955* B174045

Acknowledgments
Bradford on Avon Preservation Trust; The Dewey Museum, Warminster;
Melksham and District Historical Society; Trowbridge Museum; West
Wiltshire District Council and Wiltshire County Library. Particular thanks to
Chris Penny, David Stokes, Margaret Dobson, Jack Field, Steve Hobbs, Colin
Johns, Robin Wilson, Ivan Turtle, Tony Fivash and Kathleen Berry for their
expertise and help.

CONTENTS

FRANCIS FRITH
VICTORIAN PIONEER

FRANCIS FRITH, founder of the world-famous photographic archive, was a complex and multi-talented man. A devout Quaker and a highly successful Victorian businessman, he was philosophic by nature and pioneering in outlook.

By 1855 he had already established a wholesale grocery business in Liverpool, and sold it for the astonishing sum of £200,000, which is the equivalent today of over £15,000,000. Now a multi-millionaire, he was able to indulge his passion for travel. As a child he had pored over travel books written by early explorers, and his fancy and imagination had been stirred by family holidays to the sublime mountain regions of Wales and Scotland. 'What a land of spirit-stirring and enriching scenes and places!' he had written. He was to return to these scenes of grandeur in later years to 'recapture the thousands of vivid and tender memories', but with a different purpose. Now in his thirties, and captivated by the new science of photography, Frith set out on a series of pioneering journeys up the Nile and to the Near East that occupied him from 1856 until 1860.

INTRIGUE AND EXPLORATION

These far-flung journeys were packed with intrigue and adventure. In his life story, written when he was sixty-three, Frith tells of being held captive by bandits, and of fighting 'an awful midnight battle to the very point of surrender with a deadly pack of hungry, wild dogs'. Wearing flowing Arab costume, Frith arrived at Akaba by camel seventy years before Lawrence of Arabia, where he encountered 'desert princes and rival sheikhs, blazing with jewel-hilted swords'.

He was the first photographer to venture beyond the sixth cataract of the Nile. Africa was still the mysterious 'Dark Continent', and Stanley and Livingstone's historic meeting was a decade into the future. The conditions for picture taking confound belief. He laboured for hours in his wicker dark-room in the sweltering heat of the desert, while the volatile chemicals fizzed dangerously in their trays. Back in London he exhibited his photographs and was 'rapturously cheered' by members of the Royal Society. His reputation as a photographer was made overnight.

VENTURE OF A LIFE-TIME

Characteristically, Frith quickly spotted the opportunity to create a new business as a specialist publisher of photographs. He lived in an era of immense and sometimes violent change.

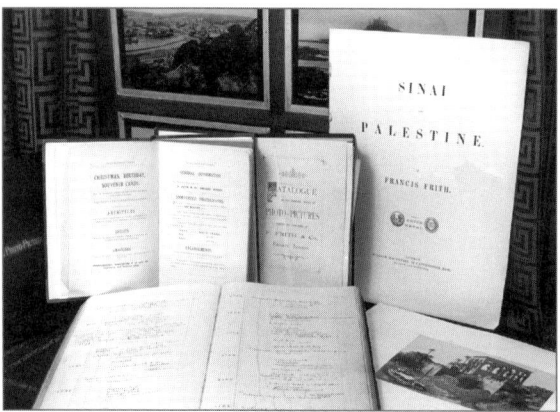

For the poor in the early part of Victoria's reign work was exhausting and the hours long, and people had precious little free time to enjoy themselves. Most had no transport other than a cart or gig at their disposal, and rarely travelled far beyond the boundaries of their own town or village. However, by the 1870s the railways had threaded their way across the country, and Bank Holidays and half-day Saturdays had been made obligatory by Act of Parliament. All of a sudden the working man and his family were able to enjoy days out and see a little more of the world.

With typical business acumen, Francis Frith foresaw that these new tourists would enjoy having souvenirs to commemorate their days out. In 1860 he married Mary Ann Rosling and set out on a new career: his aim was to photograph every city, town and village in Britain. For the next thirty years he travelled the country by train and by pony and trap, producing fine photographs of seaside resorts and beauty spots that were keenly bought by millions of Victorians. These prints were painstakingly pasted into family albums and pored over during the dark nights of winter, rekindling precious memories of summer excursions.

THE RISE OF FRITH & CO

Frith's studio was soon supplying retail shops all over the country. To meet the demand he gath-

ered about him a small team of photographers, and published the work of independent artist-photographers of the calibre of Roger Fenton and Francis Bedford. In order to gain some understanding of the scale of Frith's business one only has to look at the catalogue issued by Frith & Co in 1886: it runs to some 670 pages, listing not only many thousands of views of the British Isles but also many photographs of most European countries, and China, Japan, the USA and Canada - note the sample page shown here from the hand-written Frith & Co ledgers recording the pictures. By 1890 Frith had created the greatest specialist photographic publishing company in the world, with over 2,000 sales outlets - more than the combined number that Boots and WH Smith have today! The picture on the next page shows the Frith & Co display board at Ingleton in the Yorkshire Dales. Beautifully constructed with mahogany frame and gilt inserts, it could display up to a dozen local scenes.

POSTCARD BONANZA

The ever-popular holiday postcard we know today took many years to develop. In 1870 the Post Office issued the first plain cards, with a pre-printed stamp on one face. In 1894 they allowed other publishers' cards to be sent through the mail with an attached adhesive half-penny stamp. Demand grew rapidly, and in 1895 a new size of postcard was permitted called the court card, but there was little room for illustration. In 1899, a year after Frith's death, a new card measuring 5.5 x 3.5 inches became the standard format, but it was not until 1902 that the divided back came into being, so that the address and message could be on one face and a full-size illustration on the other. Frith & Co were in the vanguard of postcard development: Frith's sons Eustace and Cyril continued their father's monumental task, expanding the number of views offered to the public and recording more and more places in Britain, as the coasts and countryside were opened up to mass travel.

Francis Frith had died in 1898 at his villa in Cannes, his great project still growing. The archive he created continued in business for another seventy years. By 1970 it contained over a third of a million pictures showing 7,000 British towns and villages.

FRANCIS FRITH'S LEGACY

Frith's legacy to us today is of immense significance and value, for the magnificent archive of evocative photographs he created provides a unique record of change in the cities, towns and villages throughout Britain over a century and more. Frith and his fellow studio photographers revisited locations many times down the years to update their views, compiling for us an enthralling and colourful pageant of British life and character.

We are fortunate that Frith was dedicated to recording the minutiae of everyday life. For it is this sheer wealth of visual data, the painstaking chronicle of changes in dress, transport, street layouts, buildings, housing, engineering and landscape that captivates us so much today. His remarkable images offer us a powerful link with the past and with the lives of our ancestors.

THE VALUE OF THE ARCHIVE TODAY

Computers have now made it possible for Frith's many thousands of images to be accessed almost instantly. Frith's images are increasingly used as visual resources, by social historians, by researchers into genealogy and ancestry, by architects and town planners, and by teachers involved in local history projects.

In addition, the archive offers every one of us an opportunity to examine the places where we and our families have lived and worked down the years. Highly successful in Frith's own era, the archive is now, a century and more on, entering a new phase of popularity. Historians consider the Francis Frith Collection to be of prime national importance. It is the only archive of its kind remaining in private ownership. Francis Frith's archive is now housed in an historic timber barn in the beautiful village of Teffont in Wiltshire. Its founder would not recognize the archive office as it is today. In place of the many thousands of dusty boxes containing glass plate negatives and an all-pervading odour of photographic chemicals, there are now ranks of computer screens. He would be amazed to watch his images travelling round the world at unimaginable speeds through internet lines.

The archive's future is both bright and exciting. Francis Frith, with his unshakeable belief in making photographs available to the greatest number of people, would undoubtedly approve of what is being done today with his lifetime's work. His photographs depicting our shared past are now bringing pleasure and enlightenment to millions around the world a century and more after his death.

WEST WILTSHIRE TOWNS
AN INTRODUCTION

A G BRADLEY WROTE in 1909 that 'no county represents Old England without its many disadvantages more thoroughly than Wiltshire does today'. Whilst it has undoubtedly developed and changed over the last century, Wiltshire has avoided over-industrialisation, the over-commercialism of towns and the despoiling of the countryside. It retains its stunning scenery along with its unique heritage of ancient monuments and varied domestic and church architecture for locals and visitors to enjoy.

Wiltshire county (excluding Swindon Borough) is larger than the average county, but it has a smaller than average population of about 434,000 inhabitants. Its chalk downlands and fertile lower greensand have made sheep and dairy farming staple industries over the centuries. West Wiltshire is made up of the area which includes the towns of Melksham, Bradford on Avon, Trowbridge, Westbury and Warminster. With a total population of about 118,000, it is administered by the District Council, which was formed in 1974.

This part of the county is the heart of the ancient Saxon kingdom of Wessex, which controlled the West Country from the 6th century.

BRADFORD-ON-AVON, *The Bridge 1900* 45374

10

During the 9th century, the kingdom extended its rule over England south of the Thames. Under King Alfred, the kingdoms of Wessex and Mercia united to fight their common enemy, the Danes.

Wessex was divided into administrative regions called 'shires' (shares from a larger domain), and Wiltshire emerged as one of the six principal shires. Its Saxon origins are evident in place-name endings such as '-ham', as in Melksham, meaning 'a settlement', and '-bury', as in Westbury, meaning 'a clearing or enclosure'. Bradford on Avon comes from the Old English 'bradenforda be afne', meaning 'the broad ford on the river', and Trowbridge from 'treowbrycg', meaning 'tree-bridge', whilst Warminster comes from 'worian mynster', 'the church on the river Were'.

In his 'Tour through the Whole of the British Isles' written between 1724 and 1728, Daniel Defoe highlighted the importance of the clothing trade in this part of the county. Acknowledging the importance of the River Avon, 'a noble and large fresh river, branching itself into many parts', he mentioned 'Trubridge (sic) and Bradford, which are the two most eminent cloathing towns in that part of the vale'. As he moved south to Westbury and Warminster through Bradford on Avon, he wrote 'the same trade continues, the finest medley of Spanish cloths, not in England only, but in the whole world, are made in this part.'

In the west corner of the county, on the Somerset border, stands Bradford on Avon; it has been described as 'more Somerset than Wiltshire' because of its architecture and use of Bath stone. The town straddles the River Avon where the river runs westward eight miles south-east of Bath, and rises in tiers up the slopes above. Its prosperity and range of fine buildings reflect the legacy of the wool trade, and later of the rubber industry. Traffic apart, its compact layout and the development of riverside walk-ways and Country Park provide a wealth of interest for the casual and more serious walker. The town's commitment to conservation work has helped to make Bradford on Avon one of the most visited and photographed places in the county and a popular spot for overseas visitors.

To the north-west is Melksham, a working market town lying in the broad flat valley of the Wiltshire Avon where it flows from north to south. The town grew from a small village in the clearing of a large forest once used for hunting by the Plantagenet kings; the abbess and nuns of Lacock Abbey also had the right to collect wood. Oaks from Melksham Forest were used to make stalls for Salisbury Cathedral. Apart from agriculture, the main industry here was cloth weaving. When that ended in the late 19th century, rubber goods, engineering and rope-making were some of the industries that took the town into the 20th century. Attempts to develop the town as a spa town in 1815 when saline and chalybeate springs were discovered are still evident in the spa houses on Bowerhill. Today there is a renewed interest in this aspect of Melksham's history, and this is apparent in current restoration work of a Regency terrace in Spa Road.

Trowbridge is the county town, located at the centre of the group of the five West Wiltshire towns. It is the third largest town in the county, with a population of about 25,000. Although motor vehicles dominate, and all roads seem to lead to County Hall, the town can boast some fine Georgian houses, reminders of its prosperity from the cloth trade in the 18th and 19th centuries. Trowbridge was fortunate enough to have access to the coal fields of Somerset, and steam power brought tremendous expansion to the textile industry. It is not surprising that Trowbridge was known as 'the Manchester of the West' in the 19th century. Brewing, bacon curing and sausage making, along with bedding manufacture, were also industries that gave Trowbridge prominence and contributed to its economic success into the 20th century.

Close to the Somerset border, on the western edge of Salisbury Plain, stands Westbury. Because of its position beneath Salisbury Plain it has sometimes been called Westbury-under-the Playne. The main Trowbridge to Warminster road runs north to south through the centre. The rich chalky land and the abundance of water around Westbury have provided locals with a livelihood from before the time the Romans came: there is evidence of Iron Age and Bronze Age settlements. On the Bratton Road out of Westbury is the White Horse, the oldest chalk cut figure in Wiltshire, situated below the old Bratton Castle or Camp, an Iron Age hill fort.

A few miles south at the foot of the downs, near the north-west corner of Salisbury Plain, Warminster lies in the valley of the River Wylie. A market town since the 13th century, its fame was well established by the 16th century. William Cobbett was very complimentary about the place in his 'Rural Rides' in 1826, saying that it is 'a very nice town: every thing belonging to it is solid and good'. Cobbett continued: 'It is a great corn-market: one of the greatest in this part of England.' He was also a great meat connoisseur: 'I never saw veal and lamb half so fine as what I saw at Warminster'. From cloth, corn and meat to beer, iron and silk, the various trades and industries have provided locals with employment over the centuries. With its impressive long main street which runs the length of the town, its magnificent parish church, its 18th-century grammar school and its obelisk, it is a place worth exploring.

From the simplicity of the Saxon church in Bradford on Avon and the dramatic image of the chalk horse at Westbury, we can travel to the ornate splendour of Longleat House, the home of the Thynne family. West Wiltshire offers a wide variety of natural and man-made monuments to the glory of God and the celebration of man's achievements.

BRADFORD-ON-AVON, *Barton Bridge 1914* 66621

MELKSHAM & BRADFORD-ON-AVON
FROM WOOL TO WASHERS

FOR MANY YEARS, after the decline of the weaving industry, the manufacture of rubber linked the two West Wiltshire towns of Bradford on Avon and Melksham. Although the main factory business of Avon Rubber is now in Semington, Cooper Avon Tyres, a subsidiary, still dominates Melksham. The last vestiges of the same industry in Bradford on Avon (it produced, among others things, the rubber washers used worldwide in aerosol cans) are about to undergo commercial and residential development on the Kingston Mill site. Hand in hand with the new commercial enterprises go the preservation and renovation of the old. Both towns are very conscious of their responsibility to preserve and promote their heritage.

MELKSHAM, *Canon Square and the War Memorial c1955* M164004

When the vicar, Canon Wyld, lost his son in the First World War, he helped fund this memorial. The upper plinth was added to record Second World War losses. The cobbles and tree are no longer there. The weavers' cottages on the left were originally thatched; they date from late 15th century, and have undergone different facelifts over the centuries.

▶ **MELKSHAM**
St Michael's Church c1955
M164007

Pevsner writes: 'The church is out of the way to the west of the High Street, and what is attractive as a setting is around it and has little do with the town'. The church of St Michael and All Angels is entered through a picturesque iron gate with lamp.

▼ **MELKSHAM**
St Michael's Church c1955
M164002

This magnificent church, now mainly Perpendicular, dates back to Norman times – the evidence for this can be seen in wall friezes and arcading in the chancel. The tower was originally in the centre, but it was moved to the west end in 1845 by T H Wyatt. Pevsner describes the bell tower as having 'a very pretty composition of the bell-openings'.

▶ **MELKSHAM**
An Old Yew Tree in St Michael's Churchyard c1955
M164008

This view, taken from Canon Square, looks towards the churchyard and the north entrance. The ancient yew tree, propped up by poles, has reduced in size over the years. The churchyard has 43 chest tombs, which along with the two gates have had Grade II listed status since 1985.

◄ **MELKSHAM**
*Church Walk
c1955* M164003

This fine street is part of a local conservation area. It used to be called Canhold Lane. On the left, No 5, the house with the centre gable and timber frame, is 16th-century. A local map of 1543 records its original jettied gable. Nos 7 and 9 were once part of a large house; the left-hand part dates from the 18th century.

▶ **MELKSHAM**
High Street c1950
M164006

The Kings Arms Hotel (right), built in 1750, was a stop for the changing of horses and the collection of post on the London to Bristol route. Lloyds Bank (left), built in Bath stone by Rendells & Son of Devizes in Tudor style in 1922, was designed by the bank's building inspector at Salisbury.

◀ **MELKSHAM**
The Roundabout c1950 M164005

This is a busy junction leading from the Market Place, left to Spa Road, and right to King Street. Cleverlys the cycle agent (far right) is now a video shop. Stringer Automobile Engineers (left), part of which is now the Aqualeisure sports shop, used to be known as The Limes; it was bought in the 1880s by Dr Keir, who practised there with his son for many years.

▲ **MELKSHAM,** *Forest Road c1950* M164009

This view looks north-east towards Bowden Hill. The houses on the left are known as Woodrow Terrace, and the ones on the right Blackmore Terrace. They were built by Spencer's Engineering Works, which moved to Beanacre Road in 1903.

◀ **MELKSHAM**
The Hospital c1950
M164010

This hospital was built as a replacement for the cottage hospital in Bank Street. Mrs Ludlow Bruges of Seend was the benefactor who gave the hospital to the town. It was opened by the Marquis of Bath on 23 July 1938. In the grounds on the right were cottages for the ambulance driver and the gardener.

BRADFORD-ON-AVON
General View 1900
45368

This view from Grip Wood looks down on the town. The full panorama includes the spire of Christchurch in the distance and Barton Bridge, crossing the Avon, in the foreground. The railway line bisects the town east to west.

BRADFORD-ON-AVON, *Barton Bridge 1914* 66621

This view captures the essence of the town. Its landmark features are the ancient Barton Bridge in the centre, also known as Packhorse Bridge, and the spire of the parish church of Holy Trinity to the left. The area of pollarded trees has been developed into the countryside park.

BRADFORD-ON-AVON
Barton Bridge 1914
66636a

How clean the paved area of the bridge looks! Today it is in need of cleaning and restoration - the work will take place in 2003. The Rowing and Canoeing Club house can be seen behind the trees on the left. Today we can also see the remains of a World War II bunker.

BRADFORD-ON-AVON, *Barton Bridge c1950* B174024

The cutwater buttresses against the piers indicate the upstream side of the bridge. It is still a popular fishing place. We can see the corner of the West Barn on the left of the picture

◄ **BRADFORD-ON-AVON**
*A View near the Old
Tithe Barn 1900* 45386

This peaceful scene, taken
from the Packhorse Bridge,
looks towards Grip Wood.
The skyline today is heavily
brambled, but the
prominent single tree is still
recognisable. Boats moored
by the Rowing and Canoeing
Club are visible on the right.

◄ **BRADFORD-ON-AVON**
The View from the Bridge c1945 B174019

In the foreground is Barton Farm, a dairy farm worked by the Chard family. The hay ricks and the milking sheds (skillins) remind us of another time. The County Council bought the land in the 1970s for development into the Country Park. The railway goods shed (left of centre) was demolished to make a car park. The roof of the Tithe Barn is bottom left.

▲ **BRADFORD-ON-AVON,** *The View from the Quarry c1955* B174017

Only the steam train (centre) interrupts the tranquillity of this scene. This view from Grip Wood shows the rear of the Tithe Barn, which defines the southern edge of Barton Manor Farm. In the current town guide, Roger Jones informs us that '(it) is stunning; it is built of stone over 168 feet long with a massive timbered roof spanning 33 feet beneath stone tiles weighing 100 tons ... this splendid building inspires the same sort of awe-struck feeling as entering one of our great cathedrals'.

◄ **BRADFORD-ON-AVON**
The Old Tithe Barn 1900 45385

The Great Barn, or Tithe Barn, is part of Barton Manor Farm, which comprises 8 or 9 buildings grouped around a large open courtyard. According to 'The Historic Building Survey' of 1998, the barn complex was scheduled an Ancient Monument in 1930, with Listed Building status given to the adjacent buildings. Pevsner describes the 15th-century granary (left) as 'a tour-de-force without the monumental simplicity of the barn'. It is now restored and houses a pine furniture business. To the far right is the end of the West Barn (possibly late 13th-century), which appeared in the English Heritage 'at risk' register in June 2001. Restoration has now been completed by Bradford on Avon Preservation Trust.

BRADFORD-ON-AVON
The Tithe Barn c1950
B174030

Notice the cross-shaped ventilation holes known as 'oilets' on the porches. The huge oak doors are worth a close look: the heavy planks are held together by large iron hinges and large-headed nails. The interior features are remarkable, particularly the cruck-frame roof structure.

BRADFORD-ON-AVON, *The Chapel and the Bridge c1950* B174068
This view up St Margaret's Street shows two fine Georgian buildings: the one on the left has a Tuscan-columned doorway, and the one on the right is Westbury House. Just behind, at the entrance to St Margaret's Hall, we can see the petrol pumps of Stamper's Garages Ltd. The entrance to the public gardens and former swimming pool and baths is bottom left.

BRADFORD-ON-AVON
The Three Gables c1955
B174086

The Westbury Restaurant (left) was formerly Howard W Phillips, a baker's, and is now the Georgian Lodge Restaurant. The 17th-century Three Gables tea rooms is now being restored and refitted. Bradford Urban District Council took over Westbury House (right), once the scene of ugly incidents in 1791 when cloth workers clashed with the owner, a clothier named Joseph Phelps, over the use of new machinery.

BRADFORD-ON-AVON, *The Memorial and Westbury House c1955* B174090

The Town Clock (also known as the Coronation Clock) on Westbury House was removed in the 1970s. It was remounted on St Margaret's Hall to celebrate the Queen's Golden Jubilee. Pevsner describes the house thus: 'At once a fine sight … Early Georgian towards the bridge with a Palladian garden alcove to its right (with) four Tuscan columns carrying a pediment'. This part now houses the Tourist Information Centre; the ivy has been cleared to reveal the original door.

▼ **BRADFORD-ON-AVON,** *Memorial Gardens c1955* B1740106

Behind the war memorial is the terraced Festival Garden designed and planted in 1951. It has now been rededicated for the millennium and boasts a peace sculpture (known locally as 'Milly') by local artist John Willats.

▶ **BRADFORD-ON-AVON**
The Bridge 1900 45374

In his 'Topographical Collections' of 1659-70, John Aubrey wrote: 'Here is a strong and handsome bridge in the middest of which is a little chapell as at Bathe, for Masse'. Possibly built for pilgrims, the building was used as the town lock-up. Some amazing metal lavatories can be seen inside on Heritage Open Day each year.

◀ **BRADFORD-ON-AVON**
The Bridge 1900 45371

This traffic-free view of the town centre from Bridge Street conveys the history and feel of the place instantly. Much remains the same, having escaped the 1960s developers' heavy hands. The car has had the most effect in changing the town's ambience.

▶ **BRADFORD-ON-AVON**
The Bridge 1914 66622

It is obviously safe for the young man in the cap and high starched collar to stroll across the bridge. Just behind him is the Lamb Inn, which closed the year this photograph was taken. In the centre we can see the chimney-stack of Spencers Brewery, which was later taken over by Ushers.

BRADFORD-ON-AVON
The Bridge c1945
B174016

Not only has the motor car started to feature in the town, but the 'new' industries are represented by the Kingston Mill site (right), which was built for George Spencer Moulton in the 1920s on the Lamb Inn site. It was originally designed as four storeys. It is a concrete-framed building with a stone front on two sides, attempting to imitate Georgian ashlar.

▶ **BRADFORD-ON-AVON**
*Abbey Mill and Tory
c1955* B174075

Abbey Mill reminds us of the cloth industry which created the town's wealth. The mill was built in 1875 by Richard Gane, one of a family of Trowbridge mill builders. The architectural historian Julian Orbach is enthusiastic about it: 'one of the finest mill buildings of its time... Gothic detail applied without ostentation'. It closed in 1902 and re-opened in 1915 for the production of rubber goods; it has now been converted into luxury apartments.

◀ **BRADFORD-ON-AVON**
*The Bridge and the
Chapel c1960* B174021

This must be one of the most photographed landmarks in West Wiltshire. The Frith photographers obviously found its appeal irresistible. Pevsner's description seems rather mundane: 'Nine arches, plain parapet, essentially c17, though there are still two c13 arches'. The chapel is 'in the middle set on a cutwater (the angular edge of a bridge pier) with its domed roof and bell finial'.

▲ **BRADFORD-ON-AVON,** *Market Street 1900* 45377

The White Hart Temperance Hotel (centre) became Knees china and glass store in 1908, but was demolished in 1967. The Royal Oak (centre right) now houses Tillions. The glass shades on the Bradford Boot and Shoe Exchange (left) carry interesting advertisements: men's nailed boots cost from 3s 11d. Willson's the chemists (far right, opposite) has a brass pestle and mortar over the door. The building was demolished to make an entrance to Lamb Yard.

◄ **BRADFORD-ON-AVON**
Market Street c1955
B174067

This view shows the rear of the Swan Hotel on the left and the remarkable turret of the Town Hall rising above it. Pevsner describes the building as 'large, with an angle turret, Jacobean with shaped gables and mullioned and transomed windows, irregular and picturesque, but on a scale excessive for Bradford.'

▼ **BRADFORD-ON-AVON,** *The Town Hall 1900* 45375

The changing face of the Swan Hotel is displayed in the next sequence of photographs. The Town Hall was designed in 1855 by the Bath architect Thomas Fuller – he later emigrated to Canada. He won a competition for the design of the Houses of Parliament in Ottawa, and became Chief Architect of Canada.

▶ **BRADFORD-ON-AVON**
The Town Hall 1914
66624

The Swan Hotel boasts some fancy ironwork (left) advertising its new amenities. The Town Hall's various uses over the years reflect the changing needs of the townspeople. The words 'Superintendent' and 'Police' carved over the doors on the right are evidence of its history. It was council offices until 1910, and then a cinema for a while, before becoming a church.

◀ **BRADFORD-ON-AVON**
Church Street c1945
B174012

The iron horse trough was erected in 1919 as a memorial to Lieutenant Howard H Dainton and friends of the 4th Gloucesters, who died in the Great War. Notice the feet in the shape of shire-horse hooves: this was a tribute to the part played by horses in the town's economy. The trough was removed soon after the war.

▶ **BRADFORD-ON-AVON**
Market Street c1950
B174051

The billboard on the right of the Town Hall advertises 'The Wicked Lady' starring Margaret Lockwood and James Mason, showing at the Alexander Picture Theatre (in St Margaret's Hall). In June 1955, the Town Hall was inaugurated as the Roman Catholic Church of St Thomas More. Madame Soul, right, is now the Stroud and Gloucester Building Society. Nichols and Bushell, premier grocers (next door), is now the Dandy Lion.

► **BRADFORD-ON-AVON**
Market Street c1950
B174025

This view down Market Street shows the 18th-century terrace of four shops known as Pippet Buildings (right) before they were bought by the Bradford on Avon Preservation Trust in 1982. Margaret Dobson describes the work undertaken in her book 'Bradford Voices', and illustrates the remarkable transformation.

◄**BRADFORD-ON-AVON**
Market Street c1955
B174048

The sign for W E Williams Ltd, a well-known draper's store in the town, is prominent on the left. Next door at No 33 is Uncles & Son, boot makers - their delivery van is parked outside. Cobbler's materials, polish and letterheads from the shop are on display in the museum.

▲ **BRADFORD-ON-AVON,** *The Swan Hotel c1955* B174081

The post office at the entrance to the Shambles (centre) was built in 1901. It is a fine example of early 20th-century architecture, with echoes of the past in the corner oriel window. A Preservation Society Trust plaque on the wall remarks on the rare Edward VIII 1936 monogram added later to the façade.

◄**BRADFORD-ON-AVON**
The Shambles c1955
B174060

This view looks from Coppice Hill through to Market Street. The electricity show room is now Tillions glass and china shop. The 15th-century arched doorway (centre left), once entrance to the town jail, is worth a look. Notice the sign reading 'A Davis & Sons, Fish, Fruit & Potato' painted on the wall further along on the right.

BRADFORD-ON-AVON
The Shambles c1945 B174013

The Shambles connects Market Street with Silver Street. It was the site of the medieval market, and
'shambles' was the common name associated with meat trading. Notice the lamp and sign for
Payne's, the silversmith's and jeweller's (left), and the signs on the right, which show the variety of
services and goods on offer at the half-timbered shop which is now Banks bread shop.

BRADFORD-ON-AVON
Silver Street c1945 B174015

We are looking down from The Cut at the corner of Whitehead Lane (right). The signs for the Bunch
of Grapes, established in 1832, can be seen on the right.

BRADFORD-ON-AVON
Silver Street 1900 45376

The New Bear Hotel, left, is now Silver Street House, having been restored by Bradford on Avon Preservation Trust in 1977. Pevsner describes it somewhat lyrically for him: 'On the first floor, a nice rhythm of window pediments and niches'. At the centre of the photograph is E Hunt the draper's; still with the railings, it is now CR Timber Associates.

BRADFORD-ON-AVON, *Silver Street c1955* B174022

On the left, next to the only brick façade in town, is J F Goodall, linen draper and outfitter. Stockings, corsets and buttons from the old shop are on display in the museum. To the right, on the corner of Kingston Road, is R E Christopher, chemists since 1863 (the premises now belong to Davies & Davies, estate agents). The town museum agreed to buy everything from the shop, including contents and fittings, when the owner Miss Angela Christopher retired in May 1986. Visit the museum and step back in time among the mahogany counters, the coloured bottles and rows of medicines. A faint smell of 'Christopher's Famous Oriental Curry Powder, prepared from the finest spices freshly ground' permeates the exhibit.

BRADFORD-ON-AVON
The View from Tory
c1955 B174046

This view looks across towards the Trowbridge Road centre. Housing developments in the distance have changed this vista. The former Fitzmaurice Grammar School (top right corner) has given its name to one of the closes.

BRADFORD-ON-AVON, *The River Avon 1914* 66623A

The round house on the north bank of the river was a popular bathing spot. It stood in a riverside field belonging to Belcombe Court, the home of the Yerbury family, wealthy clothiers, who lived there until 1903.

▼ **BRADFORD-ON-AVON,** *The Footbridge c1965* B174101

Margaret Dobson's book 'Bradford Voices' has a picture of the pre-stressed concrete sections being lowered into place in October 1962. This bridge provided much-needed access to other parts of the town, which had only been accessible by the town bridge before.

▶ **BRADFORD-ON-AVON**
The Parish Church and the Vicarage 1914
66630a

No longer the vicarage, this is now a residence called Kingston Place. The lawns go down to the river, and the grounds can be viewed from Riverside Walk on the opposite bank of the Avon.

◀ **BRADFORD-ON-AVON**
The Parish Church
1914 66630

Arthur Mee described Holy Trinity Church as 'a fine church with many fine possessions'. On the wall of the nave is 'one of the loveliest fragments of sculpture in Wiltshire, the portrait of a 13th-century lady, with curls in her hair, and hands clasped'. This was rescued during renovation work in the 1860s - it had been used, face down, to repair paving.

▶ **BRADFORD-ON-AVON**
Holy Trinity Church
1900 45378

This shows the south entrance to the church, which Pevsner describes thus: 'Perpendicular also s porch (with a niche) and the embattled s chapel with straight-headed windows'. Over the door are painted words from Psalm 84.

BRADFORD-ON-AVON
Holy Trinity Church c1955 B174026

Here the secular and the sacred are close together. The 19th-century Abbey Mill contrasts with the
15th-century church tower, which possibly replaced a smaller Norman one. In his 'Bradford on
Avon Past and Present', Harold Fassnidge describes the carillon, dating from 1614, as having been
augmented over the years; it now has a repertoire of hymns played regularly.

BRADFORD-ON-AVON
*Holy Trinity Church
1900* 45379

The interior has been altered over the years; here the choir stalls are still in place. The monument on the left of the chancel arch is to Samuel Cam 1714 –1792, a prominent clothier of Chantry House. The draped marble urn can be viewed by the congregation, and, as Rosemary F Carr comments in her book 'Storied Urns', 'it is a constant reminder of the mortality of man'.

BRADFORD-ON-AVON, *St Laurence's Saxon Chapel 1900* 45381

This Saxon church had been concealed by sheds and buildings for many centuries. It was re-discovered by Canon W H R Jones, the vicar of Holy Trinity and a keen antiquarian. He came across references to it in a text dated 1125. Excavations outside revealed the walls, and repairs revealed the carvings. A table made from one of the old oak beams from the 1850 restoration work is on show in the town museum.

BRADFORD-ON-AVON
St Laurence's Saxon Chapel, The Interior 1900 45383

John Chandler and Derek Parker describe the effect of the church on the visitor in 'Wiltshire
Churches, an Illustrated History': 'There is an aura of intense mystery, and to submit to its darkness
by entering on a sunny day can be a profoundly awesome experience'.

BRADFORD-ON-AVON
St Laurence's Saxon Chapel, The Interior 1900 45384

Arthur Mee in his King's England series says about the church: 'It is naked and bare, and all the better for that'. The chancel arch, which we see here, is the narrowest in England at 3ft 6in. The walls are 2ft 5in thick, and the decorations were all cut by Saxon masons.

43

▲ **BRADFORD-ON-AVON**
The Saxon Church c1950 B174033

The simplicity and to some extent austerity of St Laurence's contrasts with the richness of Holy Trinity. We are not used to churches without stained glass windows, or in fact without windows at all. This church would have been lit by candles.

BRADFORD-ON-AVON ▶
Christ Church 1914 66636

This view, taken from Mason's Lane, shows the church on the hill, which was built in 1841 by Manners of Bath. Pevsner describes it as 'a big, prosperous church with a west tower carrying a recessed spire. Flying buttresses support the spire'. In the middle of the road is the turreted turnpike weighbridge with splendid lamp on top, used until 1931.

BRADFORD-ON-AVON
Christ Church c1950 B174023

By 1839, the parish church of Holy Trinity was becoming a little run down. This church, built in
1841 on the Bath/Winsley Road, proclaimed the wealth and status of the local residents at the time
with its size and its landmark steeple.

BRADFORD-ON-AVON
An Old Cottage 1914
66638

Known locally as Witches'
Cottage, it is thatched in
this photograph with long
straw. Today it has been re-
thatched in combed wheat,
which gives a smoother
appearance. The only
thatched property in
Bradford on Avon, it is
thought to have been built
as a rustic folly in the
grounds of The Priory.

BRADFORD-ON-AVON, *The Priory 1914* 66633

The intriguing porch embellishments have been lost, sad to say. The only part left of this superb medieval mansion is the
1820s extension on the left. The place fell into disrepair, and bits were sold off in the 1930s.

BRADFORD-ON-AVON
The Old Priory 1900
45380

The Rev W H Jones in his 'History of Bradford on Avon', published by Wm Dotesio in 1907, writes: 'The nucleus of this fine old house dates probably from the 15th century and its founder was a Rogers, most likely the serjeant at law'. Dramatic effects were created by features such as the oriel window (right) and the moulded stone parapet and crenellations.

BRADFORD-ON-AVON, *The Hall c1950* B174018

Pevsner described The Hall as 'the one nationally major mansion in Bradford, not a town house but a country house in character'. It was built in 1610 by John Hall, a clothier; in 1847 it became the home of the Moulton family, who founded the rubber manufacturing business. Currently it is the home of Dr Alex Moulton, inventor of the small-wheeled Moulton bicycle.

▶ **BRADFORD-ON-AVON**
*The View from Winsley
Road c1955* B174045

This view looks across to
the Trowbridge Road - its
strong line of Victorian and
Edwardian houses is
evident going into the
distance. Much of this scene
has been developed at Wine
Street on the left, and Sandy
Leaze now covers the
farmland in the foreground.

◀ **BRADFORD-ON-AVON**
The Canal 1914 66635a

This is Avoncliff, with the
aqueduct running over the
river and railway at
Avoncliff Halt. This part of
the canal has been recently
restored. The track on the
left runs from Westwood
stone quarry.

▲ **BRADFORD-ON-AVON,** *The Canal c1955* B174039

This shows Lower Wharf on the Kennet and Avon Canal, with the corner of Lock Inn Cottage Café to the bottom right and the back of the gardens of the Canal Tavern.

◄**BRADFORD-ON-AVON**
Westwood Manor 1914
66637a

Westwood Manor lies about 1½ miles south-west of Bradford. Now administered by the National Trust, it is described as 'a 15th-century stone manor house, altered in the early 17th century, with late Gothic and Jacobean windows and fine plasterwork'.

49

TROWBRIDGE
COUNTY TOWN

ARTHUR MEE describes Trowbridge as 'a handsome and ancient place, one of the fine group of old towns in which Wiltshire is so rich'. As the county town, it is the administrative centre of the region, with industrial, commercial and retail businesses in and around the town. The Wiltshire County Library Services and Museum Service and the Wiltshire Record Offices are based here, and so is the Consortium, an enterprise started in 1971 to enable county councils to order supplies such as stationery and equipment in bulk and distribute them. In spite of radical road developments and extensive building programmes over the last sixty years, there is much of architectural and historical interest to the visitor.

TROWBRIDGE, *A Composite Postcard c1965* T48075

The recipient of this card would enjoy the picturesque view of the parish church and the peaceful scenes in and around the Town Hall. It is a far cry from the busy modern centre of shops and businesses and the complex roadway around the administrative centre of County Hall.

TROWBRIDGE
The Town Hall 1907 57697d

The Town Hall was designed by A S Goodridge 1887-89 and built to celebrate Queen Victoria's Golden Jubilee. Pevsner described it as 'in a wild Franco-Elizabethan style'. It is currently used as the magistrates' court. The corner building on the left is Aplins the chemist, famous for its mineral water production as well as for its own range of medicines such as 'Aplin's Cough Balsam – the great lung healer'.

51

TROWBRIDGE
Ashton Mill 1923
73989c

At the height of the woollen industry, Ashton Mill was added to Court Mills in 1860. This became part of what was once regarded as one of the finest industrial complexes in England. The gas engines could be heard by locals as they strolled in the park.

► **TROWBRIDGE**
The Market House 1907 57697c

The Market House was designed in 1861 by the Bath architect C E Davis in Victorian Italianate style. Davis was also responsible for the discovery and excavations of the Roman baths, as well as founding the Bath School of Art. These arches, with their wonderful carvings and Biblical quotations, now form part of the entrance to Castle Place, the shopping precinct; they are worth a close look.

▼ **TROWBRIDGE**
Fore Street and the Town Hall 1900
45342

The Market Tavern, far left, now forms the entrance to the White Hart Yard. The pub doors were rescued after demolition, and are preserved in the town's museum. On the right, at No 29, Manoah Tucker, the boot and shoe maker, competes with his neighbour, the Public Benefit Boot Company, for the most impressive light fittings. At No 32 is Saxty's, tailor and hatter.

▶ **TROWBRIDGE**
Fore Street 1900
45341

The spire of the parish church of St James stands proudly among this busy commercial scene. On the corner of Fore Street and Church Walk is Knees (centre), which opened in 1879. Its signwriting boasts that it is 'The largest furnishing house in the district. Prices lower than city houses'. On the left is Avons & Sons, brush manufacturer. The three large brushes hanging over the entrance help to advertise their wares.

◀ **TROWBRIDGE**
Fore Street 1950
T84024

The George Hotel was the oldest surviving licensed house in town, dating back to the 14th century. It was closed in 1901, and the whole building was demolished. However, the 19th-century façade was retained, and the building is now shared by a bank and shoe shop.

TROWBRIDGE
Silver Street 1900 45344

A variety of signs help to advertise the range of goods and services on offer. Prominent are those of Dotesio & Todd (left), booksellers and printers. Sandwiched between the 'gents' clothing from 4/11 to 15/11' and Woodward's the hairdresser. On the right is the glass front and the lantern of Hill's Public Hall, now Mackay's. Up until the First World War it was used as a cinema, and as a venue for wrestling, boxing matches and roller skating.

▶ **TROWBRIDGE**
Silver Street
c1965 T84068a

This shows an interesting mix of 18th- and 19th-century building frontages, from H B Pitt (left) to Hill's Public Hall, now Mackays, the chemist, formerly Aplins, and the Town Hall, now the magistrates' court.

TROWBRIDGE ▶
Silver Street c1950
T84040

This view was taken before the 1960s development which involved the demolition of the New Inn (centre right) and the neighbouring Georgian buildings to build the Co-op. At No 13 is William George Butcher, the drapers (left), with its comprehensive display of ladies' underwear.

◄ **TROWBRIDGE**
Fore Street c1950
T84043

This photograph was taken outside the Town Hall, looking towards St James's parish church. H B Penty, opticians and jewellers (right) has been rebuilt now as Dorothy Perkins. Next door is a listed building, now the Portman Building Society. Built in 1855 in early Renaissance Italianate style, it has some fine carved and moulded features.

► **TROWBRIDGE**
Fore Street c1950
T84004

The Midland Bank on the left is a fine Georgian building described by Pevsner as 'amazingly stately'. To the right are rather grand mock half-timbered premises for the Electricity Supply Co. Further along on the right is the Gaumont Cinema next to Bowyers (Wiltshire Bacon Co).

TROWBRIDGE
The War Memorial 1923 73990c

The war memorial was erected at the entrance to the park and unveiled in 1923. The beginning of
the avenue of Cornish elm trees, each planted by a war widow to mark the deaths of young
Trowbridge men who died in the First World War, can be seen behind.

TROWBRIDGE
*The People's Park
1907* 57706

The grounds, which used to belong to The Limes, the big house which was the site of the Town Hall, were opened in 1884 for the locals to use. Its popularity led to their purchase by public subscription to celebrate the Queen Victoria's Golden Jubilee, and they were laid out with trees, shrubs, paths and a bandstand.

TROWBRIDGE, *The Parish Church of St James from the North-West c1955* T84017

The church of St James was probably founded in about 1200. There are rectors recorded since 1229. The church was pulled down and completely remodelled between 1460 and 1485 in the Perpendicular style. It retained the magnificent 160ft spire from the 14th century.

► **TROWBRIDGE**
St James's Church from the North-East c1955
T84028

Arthur Mee was impressed by this church, and in his
King's England series he wrote that the spire is 'a
striking spectacle with three bands of panelling round
it' and marvelled at its 'embattled tower richly
gargoyled with all manner of strange birds, beast and
demons'. The almshouses in Union Street (far left)
were built in 1861.

▼ **TROWBRIDGE**
The Parish Church, the Interior 1923 73988

In 1907, major interior works were undertaken. Organ
and choir stalls were installed, and pews were removed
and rearranged to form a central aisle. The royal arms,
painted in oils on canvas, dated c1800, are displayed
above the chancel arch. The tradition dates from
Elizabeth I, who ordered the royal arms to be set up in
churches to proclaim the Monarch supreme governor
of the Church of England.

▶ **TROWBRIDGE**
The Parade 1900
45346

This traffic-free view of the Parade shows the trees planted for the Jubilee – they were removed in the 1930s to make room for parking. The houses behind are fine examples of properties built by wealthy clothiers in the 1700s. Pevsner describes them as 'the best group of ashlar-faced houses, really a stretch of palaces'.

◀**TROWBRIDGE**
The Parade 1923
73986

Parking was not a problem in 1923. Notice the pitched paving in front of Parade House (left), where stones are embedded between 6in and 18in deep, a method used in the county. The ornate corner building (centre) is in fact an Edwardian sham, a façade to hide Ushers brewery behind.

TROWBRIDGE
Wingfield Road 1907
57701

Taken from the corner of
Westbourne Gardens, this
view shows what is now a
busy residential road.
To the left is the Catholic
church of St John the
Baptist, built in 1875 in
Decorated Gothic style.
The turreted tower of Holy
Trinity can be seen in the
distance further along.

TROWBRIDGE, *Trinity Church c1955* T84048

Known locally as 'the church on the roundabout', Trinity Church stands on its own island at the interchange of Stallard
Street, Wingfield Road and Newtown. Dating from 1838, it was built to seat more than a thousand, to cater for the growing
parish. It was reduced in size in 1908 to seat 750. Built in the Early English style, it was said to have been modelled on the
Lady Chapel at Salisbury Cathedral.

TROWBRIDGE
Holy Trinity Church c1955 T48032

The church became known as the Garrison Church in the mid 19th century, as the Royal Artillery
barracks once stood in the parish. With its vaulted ceiling, the interior has a great sense of space.
The pulpit is by C E Davis, who also designed the Market House.

TROWBRIDGE
The County Cricket Ground, the Pavilion 1907 57705

The town has had a cricket team since 1844. This pavilion was opened in 1896. In June 2001, The Wiltshire Times described it as 'one of the town's hidden treasures'. It reported that the pavilion was in desperate need of restoration, and that the Friends of Trowbridge Cricket Pavilion had received a cheque from the daughter of F W Stancomb, who had 'retained the captaincy for 50 years'.

TROWBRIDGE, *Wiltshire County Council Offices c1950* T84016

The first county council was formed in 1889, with the 4th Marquis of Bath as chairman. It used to rotate meetings around the county. After the county council had settled in Trowbridge for some years, purpose-built buildings designed by P D Hepworth were completed in 1940. Over time, the Bythesea Road site has expanded to include the County Library and Records Office.

TROWBRIDGE
*A Composite
Postcard c1965*
T84074

This card represents some other aspects of the life in and around the town in the 1960s. The popular swimming pool was built in 1939, but it was demolished to make way for Tesco's superstore. The Girls' High School, founded in 1915, is now part of the John of Gaunt School.

WESTBURY & WESTBURY LEIGH

UNDER THE EYE OF THE HORSE

THE BEAUTY of the area round Westbury, which stands on the western edge of Salisbury Plain, has remained unspoilt for centuries. The town's identity is linked to the magnificent white horse cut into the chalk hillside, a landmark which guides the traveller. The economic growth of the town and district has depended over the centuries on agriculture, especially sheep farming, the wool trade, glove-making and leather work, iron work, and cement production. More recently light engineering and commercial enterprises have become part of the business park developments. In nearby Westbury Leigh, part of the parish of Westbury, cloth mills and weavers' cottages remind us of its past.

WESTBURY, *A Composite Postcard c1965* W263043

This Frith postcard captures well the diversity of the town, from the ancient White Horse hewn out of chalk hillside and the magnificent church at the heart of the community to the commercial life of the sixties shopping parade built in brick and concrete. To the top right, we see Queen's Court with the shops and post office in Oldfield Park.

WESTBURY
The White Horse 1900 45365

This view looks south-east towards the Westbury White Horse. It was cut out of the chalk in 1778, although legend suggests that a shape facing the other way was carved out to commemorate King Alfred's defeat of the Danes in AD 878. It was remodelled in 1853 and restored twenty years later.

▼ **WESTBURY,** *The View from the White Horse c1965* W263020

The landscape of Westbury would not be complete without the landmark 400ft chimney of the Blue Circle Cement Works (now Lafarge Cement,) which opened in 1962 on the site of the former Westbury Iron Company. The elm trees in the centre unfortunately died off during the 1970s.

▶ **WESTBURY**
The White Horse c1955
W263011

On the left is the Bratton Road out of Westbury. The White Horse is the oldest in Wiltshire; it is situated below the old Bratton Castle or Camp, an Iron Age hill fort. It measures 180ft from head to tail and over 107ft from foot to shoulder; its eye circumference alone is 25 feet.

◄ **WESTBURY**
The View from the Church Tower c1965 W263031

This view across the Market Place shows the lovely old tiled roofs of a variety of buildings dating from the 18th to the early 19th century. In the foreground is the rear of the houses facing Cannon Green, and to the left is the corner of Maristow Street. The gasometer (top right) was demolished in 1988. The Meadow Lane development has changed the view at the top left.

► **WESTBURY**
Market Place c1955
W263008

The Town Hall and the First World War memorial are important focal points. A weighbridge plate can be seen between the two. Sandwiched between the Town Hall and the Lopes Arms is Perkin's Pieces, now Wessex Books and Prints. Dating from the early 18th century, it has unusual features, 'an undulating Edwardian parapet with 3 blind arches over plate glass sash windows' (The Department of Environment List of Buildings of Special Architectural or Historic Interest).

WESTBURY
The Town Centre c1950
W263009

Used for many years as a public library, the Town Hall has many features of note, such as the three-bay colonnaded ground floor divided by rusticated piers, and the arched upper windows with balustered aprons.

▶ **WESTBURY**
Market Place
c1965 W263024

Cars have begun to dominate the square here. The War Memorial was removed later to increase the parking area. The Town Hall was built in 1815 by Sir Manasseh Lopes on the site of the old Market Hall.

◀ **WESTBURY**
The Town Centre
c1950 W263010

This photograph and W263028 (pages 76-77) look across to the corner of West End and Fore Street. At the centre is Marlborough House, and then Barclays Bank (now a private residence). It is a magnificent red brick early 18th-century house with a shell-hood doorway.

▲ **WESTBURY,** *Market Place c1965* W263023

The Lopes Arms, left, became the Westbury Hotel in 1989. There has been an inn on the site since the 14th century. It became the St George and Dragon in 1596, the Lord Abingdon Arms in 1754, and the Lopes Arms after a terrible fire in 1809. The rendering has been removed to show the red brick facing. The splendid ornate wrought iron lamp bracket is still at the entrance, a reminder of the Lopes family. Cannon Green, consisting of Nos 1-3 Market Place, is an 18th-century terrace, named after the Russian cannon from the Crimean War which used to stand there before it was removed for scrap metal during the Second World War.

◀ **WESTBURY**
All Saints Church c1955 W263003

The original church probably dates from 1437. This large cruciform church in the Perpendicular style has a rectangular central tower. The low transepts were renewed and restored in 1847 by TH Wyatt. Earlier masonry was used in some parts of the ashlar construction.

WESTBURY
Market Place c1965
W263028

There has been an increase in car usage since W263010, (page 74) although little else has changed. The Crown Hotel on the left dates back to the late 18th century. Next door is Ernest Chard, chemist, now One Stop Shop. The White Lion public house (beyond) is late 18th-century.

WESTBURY
The Church c1965
W263037

The church is set in an enclosed churchyard, where there are a number of good altar tombs. The tower houses one of the heaviest peals of eight bells in the world, the second heaviest in Britain. The Department of the Environment List describes the tower thus: 'a 2 stage crenellated tower with octagonal stair turret to north-east. Steep pitched chancel roof with stone tiles'.

WESTBURY, *All Saints Church, the Interior c1955* W263018

The altar rail has been changed to a modern wooden one, and the choir stalls have been removed. The Perpendicular east window has three crucifixion panels dating from 1847 given by the Rev Stafford Brown, who was responsible for major repairs and works to the church.

WESTBURY
The Church, the Interior c1955
W263016

This view towards the altar shows the fine transverse arches with a flying buttress-like retaining arch. The intricate oak rood screen was removed in 1969. The tiled nave floor was laid in about 1867, but was replaced with carpet in 1969.

WESTBURY, *The View from the Church Tower c1965* W263032

The former primary school in the foreground now houses the White Horse Team Ministry hall and offices. Westbury House, behind, built for the Laverton family in the early 19th century, is now the library.

WESTBURY
The Church, The Interior c1965 W263042

The west end has a stained glass window donated by the mill owner Abraham Laverton in 1868. The
font is now in place at the east end.

WESTBURY
*Warminster Road
c1965* W263030

The corner of Edward Street on the right has altered considerably; the end building was demolished in 1999. The second shop along is Fred Macey's, advertising cycles and prams. On the left, H J R Perry, fruit and vegetable merchant, is now a JR Motors of Devizes.

WESTBURY, *High Street c1965* W263039

The shopping parade was built between 1960 and 1966 by Wallis, Finlay, Smith & Ball on the site of a house of some historic interest called Fountainville. The millennium project book, 'Westbury & Westbury Leigh, A Celebration of the Town & its People' details the development. Alterations to traffic priorities and new paved areas for pedestrians were made in 1992.

▼ **WESTBURY,** *High Street c1960* W263025

The first retail shop opened in January 1963. Four of the units were taken by Keymarket supermarket (right), which proved popular with locals. Phase Two had just been completed at the time of this photograph.

► **WESTBURY**
Warminster Road
c1965 W263029

Road developments have altered this view. There is a roundabout at the junction with Orchard Road on the left, and the opening to the Warminster Road car park is where the telephone box stood (right).

◄WESTBURY
Fore Street c1955
W263007

This view was taken from the Market Place. Fore Street, leading into the A350 Trowbridge Road, is now a very busy road in and out of town. The motorcyclist with sidecar looks as though he is king of the road, with no fear of any vehicle larger than a bicycle.

► WESTBURY
Oldfield Park Estate c1965
W263035

This post-war council development can be dated by the medallions which were set into the front brickwork at the time of building. The estate is still expanding, and has a new set of Groves – named after different types of trees.

WESTBURY LEIGH
The Church c1955
W264007

The Church of the Holy Saviour was built between 1876 and 1880 with money raised by the Phipps family, who had been connected to the woollen industry since the 17th century. Pevsner describes the church as 'a serious, well-done neo-Perpendicular job'. The tower was added in 1888. Today the church is part community hall and part place of worship.

◄ **WESTBURY**
*Meadow Lane
Estate c1965*
W263036

This view looks
west towards
Frogmore Road,
and shows a new
private housing
development. The
parish church of
All Saints is a
familiar landmark
in the centre
distance.

▲ **WESTBURY LEIGH,** *The Village c1955* W264001

This view shows the entrance to the Phipps Arms, formerly the Black Horse Inn. Known locally as 'the Phipper', it is currently being converted into residences. The houses were built in pre-fabricated reinforced concrete (PRC), but the façades have been altered and the turn-in extended.

◄**WESTBURY LEIGH**
The Post Office c1965
W264009

By this date the lovely
brickwork seen in W264005
(pages 86-87) had been
rendered and painted
white. The front of the
premises of the post office
and general stores has
recently been changed
with the opening up of the
front of the part behind
the telephone box.

WESTBURY LEIGH
The Village c1950
W264005

This view looks towards Leighton House on the hill. The post office and general stores in Leigh Street was, and still is, important to the community. The building opposite has been demolished, and now forms the entrance to Leigh Close.

WARMINSTER
MITTENS & MILITIA

IN HIS 'Round About Wiltshire' (1901), A G Bradley wrote about Warminster: 'its situation is the most striking feature, for that is beautiful, though there is nothing in the aspect of the town unworthy of such a sight'. The town is surrounded by green fields and woodland to the south of Salisbury Plain. The landscape of hills, barrows and earthworks remind us of the beginnings of civilisation with the Neolithic, Bronze Age and Iron Age settlements and hill forts.

Over the centuries, the town's fortunes have depended on wool, along with the corn trade and glove making. Today small businesses thrive, and the town's military connections since the 1930s are still strong. The Army Base Repair Organisation and Warminster Training Centre are based here. The population has quadrupled to nearly 20,000 since the turn of the century, and residential development continues. The southern bypass has helped the town maintain its character, and the preservation of old buildings is now a priority.

WARMINSTER, *Cley Hill c1950* W261006

We can see this beautiful view of Cley Hill to the west of the town on the Frome Road. Formerly owned by the Marquis of Bath, and now in the care of the National Trust, this Iron Age fort has two Bronze Age bowl barrows. Bonfires were lit on it at the time of the Armada.

WARMINSTER
The View from the South c1955 W261015

Taken from the football field, this view looks towards the Chapel of St Lawrence in the High Street with its 14th-century tower and early 19th-century spire. The old Regal cinema stands in front. At the centre is the children's play area in King George's Field, which was opened in 1938. There is a housing development on the top right green field area.

WARMINSTER, *Copheap and the Park c1955* W261016

Copheap Hill was bought by the town in memory of those who died in the two World Wars. It is a beautiful spot under the beeches from which to view the whole town.

WARMINSTER
*The Lake and the
Pleasure Ground c1965*
W261062

The lake, the park and the
pleasure grounds are still
popular places for locals to
visit. The park was opened in
1924, and the children's
paddling pool was added to
the King George's Field in
1947.

▶ **WARMINSTER**
The Lake and the Pleasure Ground
c1965 W261064

This view looks towards the west, and shows the boat house and bandstand. The lake is home to a variety of water fowl, including swans and coots.

◀**WARMINSTER**
The Pleasure Ground
c1950 W261004

The scene has changed little today, except for some landscaping undertaken for the Queen's Silver Jubilee in the woodland area behind the island on the left.

▲ **WARMINSTER,** *Bell Hill c1965* W261061

The Bell and Crown (left) is a very old inn dating back to 1675, and it stands on the old coaching road from London to Barnstaple. In his book 'The Inns and Taverns of Warminster', Reg Cundick writes: 'It used to have its own brewhouse. At one time the landlord had the right to put drunks in stocks on the other side of the road'. In the distance we can see Sambourne Hospital, formerly the Union Workhouse, built in 1836; it is now a residential development called The Beeches. More information on this can be found in the Dewey Museum and in the book 'Warminster in the Twentieth Century' by Celia Lane and Pauline White.

◄**WARMINSTER**
Christ Church c1955
W261014

We are looking towards the town from the Common. The market gardens in the centre are now the Wylie Road housing development. Christ Church was built in 1830-31, high above the town on Sambourne Hill.

WARMINSTER
The Market Place
c1950 W261009

The many signs help to identify businesses at this time. Bottom right is KTS Pianos, whose proprietor Rex Siminson was also organist at the minster. Next door is W H Smith and Stiles' Bros, ironmongers, with the Cleveland Oil signs. Further along are the Anchor Hotel and the Bath Arms. Opposite is the Old Bell Hotel, first recorded in 1483. Pevsner describes it as 'nicely white and black, and the ground floor colonnaded'. Corn sellers used to display their wares under cover here at the front of the hotel.

WARMINSTER
The Market Place
c1965 W261057

The Bath Arms Hotel
building dates from 1732.
Reg Cundick gives an
interesting history of it in
his book. On Barclays Bank,
left, is a sign for the
Warminster Journal, which
is still produced by Coates
and Parker next door.

WARMINSTER
The Market Place
c1950 W261025

In the middle is the hanging sign for the Three Horse Shoes, which closed about 1968. This is now the southern entrance to the Three Horse Shoes shopping complex; the entrance also leads to the central car park and the library and museum. Hibberd Bros, the drapers, is now Batemans, opticians.

▼ **WARMINSTER,** *Christ Church c1950* W261002

This church was built as part of the 'suburban' church movement for dealing with the expanding industrial towns of Wiltshire. Pevsner describes it as 'a long church, W tower with tall, heavy pinnacles. Tall two-light Perpendicular windows'. The architect was John Leachman, who was also responsible for St Margaret's, Corsley. The church was expanded c1870 by T H Wyatt.

▶ **WARMINSTER**
Christ Church c1965
W261066

The Frith photographer was standing in Upper Marsh Road to take this view, which looks across the new churchyard to the old churchyard beyond.

WARMINSTER
High Street from St Lawrence's c1965
W261065

From outside the chapel of St Lawrence, we can see the Athenaeum (centre), built in 1858 as a place of entertainment. Designed by William Jervis Stent, a non-conformist Warminster architect (he also designed the Laverton Institute in Westbury and Calne Free Church), it became the Picture Palace in 1912. It closed in 1964, but re-opened as an arts centre in 1969.

WARMINSTER
High Street c1965
W261058

The corner block on the right is Samuel Webb's drapery shop at No 27 and 28 High Street. It has an unusual hipped roof which neatly turns the corner to The Close. We can see a postman outside, struggling up the hill with his wheeled hamper of mail.

WARMINSTER
High Street c1950
W261024

The Hants and Sussex coach is parked outside Hill House, a former solicitor's home until it became a café restaurant in 1898. In 1950 the premises were run by Ted Bowmaster and his brother, and was known locally as Ted's Café. Notice the sister in her habit, strolling downhill on the right. She was probably from the town's Community of St Denys.

WARMINSTER
George Street c1965
W261060

This photograph was taken at the corner of Sambourne Road looking towards Carter's Corner, Nos 50–54A High Street and No 2 Portway, recently restored by the Warminster Preservation Trust. The terrace on the left is noteworthy: it dates from 1815 to 1830, and has interesting architectural features such as stone cill bands to the first and second floors and sash windows alternating with blind panels.

WARMINSTER
Silver Street c1965
W261059

We can see a mixture of residential and commercial premises here. The Department of the Environment's 'List of Buildings of Special Architectural or Historic Interest' notes the row of late 18th-century and early 19th-century houses on the right, with their old tiled mansard roofs and three-flue ridge chimneys.

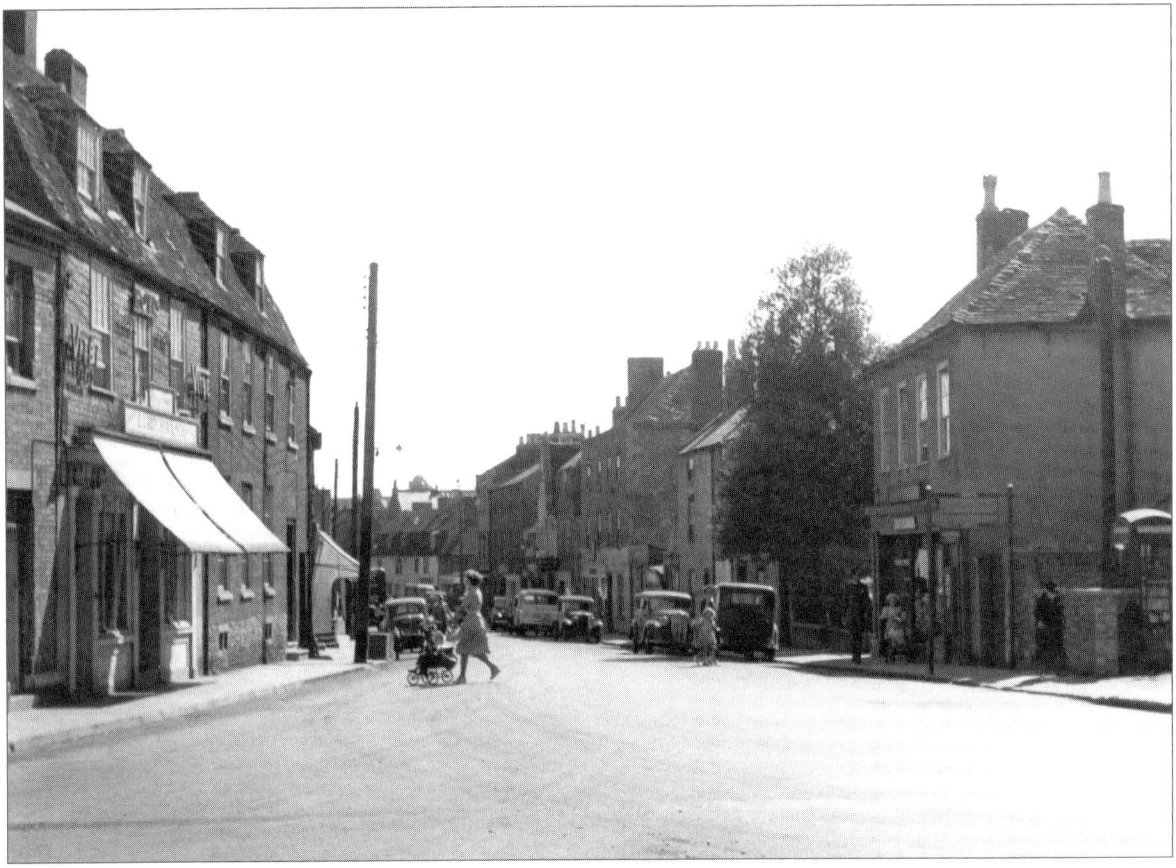

◄ **WARMINSTER**
Silver Street c1955
W261018

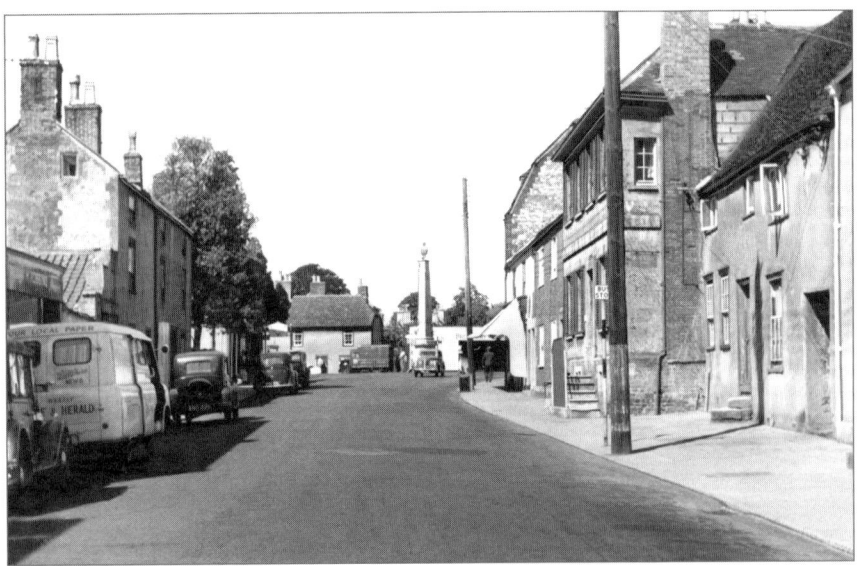

The house on the right with the double flight of moulded steps, known as The Cedars, is late 18th-century. It was formerly the girls' orphanage, part of the Community of St Denys, and then a solicitor's office from 1970 to 1994; it is now a residential home.

WARMINSTER
Silver Street
c1950 W261019

This view was taken from the Obelisk, and shows the premises of E J Butcher & Son, bakers, on the left. According to an account in 'Warminster in the Twentieth Century' by Celia Lane and Pauline White, 'Miss Lang, who lived next door at No 22, kept a pile of shoes in her bedroom to throw at the rats from the bakehouse'.

WARMINSTER, *Vicarage Street c1955* W261017

On the right are the buildings of the Community of St Denys, now part of Warminster School. At the top of the bend is the pedimented Wren House, described in the Department of the Environment's list as 'an extremely good example of an early Georgian 5-bay house circa 1720 or 1730'. It is now a retirement home.

WARMINSTER
The Obelisk c1965
W261053

This triangular Bath stone fountain stands at the junction of Silver Street, Vicarage Street and Church Street; it was erected in 1783. Danny Howell writes about it in 'The Warminster & District Archive', Winter 1988. The ornamental pineapple on top of the urn was a popular symbol of affluence in the 18th century. A lion's head spout and one of the cattle troughs still remain.

WARMINSTER
St Boniface College c1950 W261005

The Bristol architect Joseph Glascodine built the original house, the centre part, in 1796. This then
became the core of the college, which was founded in 1860 by Canon Sir James Erasmus Philipps,
vicar of Warminster 1859-1897, to educate young men as missionaries. Years later he founded
St Denys College to train young women. It was closed in 1943, and is now part of Warminster School.

WARMINSTER
Church Street c1955
W261020

In the centre we can see the former chapel of St Boniface College. The clock on the Conservative Club (left) was erected in memory of John Hall (1830-1909), who ran a local nail making and paint merchandising business. He was a pioneer of the Tariff Reform Movement in the west of England, and was opposed to the Free Trade policy.

WARMINSTER, *St Boniface College and the College Chapel c1955* W261021

This view from the west shows the right-hand wing, built in 1927 by Sir Charles Nicolson. It is described as 'quite impressive Gothic' in the Department of the Environment's list.

▼ **WARMINSTER,** *St Boniface College c1955* W261026

The left-hand wing is neo-Jacobean, and was added in 1897 by J A Reeve; it has dramatic features such as a cornice and balustraded parapet, and finials to its gabled dormers.

► **WARMINSTER**
The Minster Church of St Denys c1940 W261012

This late 14th-century church stands about half a mile north-east of the Market Place. It was thoroughly rebuilt between 1887 and 1889 by the architect Sir Arthur Blomfeld, who was responsible for restoration work at Salisbury Cathedral and also Marlborough College.

WARMINSTER
The Minster c1955
W261022

The magnificent old yew tree obscures the entrance, which is through a projecting porch. The interior has many fine features, including part of a Norman arch reused for a small window in the north transept, an octagonal pulpit with decorative tracery and inlaid marble, and a gilt and alabaster reredos.

WARMINSTER
The Shearwater Café c1960 W261033

Also known as Bargate Cottage, it is situated on the turnpike road from Crockerton to Maiden Bradley, and adjacent to Shearwater Lake, part of the Longleat estate. A recent 'To Let' advertisement in the Warminster Journal offered the place as 'a quintessentially English country Tea Rooms', claiming that 'the Bargate has served generations of local fishermen, boating and yachting enthusiasts, pony trekkers, cyclists and walkers'.

WARMINSTER
Longleat House c1955 W261029

The home of the Marquis of Bath, Longleat was built by Sir John Thynne. Dating possibly from the 1570s, it is a fine example of high Elizabethan style. The south portal entrance is 18th-century. The balustrade motif was inspired by Somerset House, which itself took elements from the 'Loire style' in France. The grounds were landscaped by Capability Brown between 1757 and 1762.

INDEX

Frith Book Co Titles

www.francisfrith.co.uk

The Frith Book Company publishes over 100 new titles each year. A selection of those currently available are listed below. For latest catalogue please contact Frith Book Co.
Town Books 96 pages, approximately 100 photos. **County and Themed Books** 128 pages, approximately 150 photos (unless specified). All titles hardback with laminated case and jacket, except those indicated pb (paperback)

Amersham, Chesham & Rickmansworth (pb)	1-85937-340-2	£9.99	Devon (pb)	1-85937-297-x	£9.99
Andover (pb)	1-85937-292-9	£9.99	Devon Churches (pb)	1-85937-250-3	£9.99
Aylesbury (pb)	1-85937-227-9	£9.99	Dorchester (pb)	1-85937-307-0	£9.99
Barnstaple (pb)	1-85937-300-3	£9.99	Dorset (pb)	1-85937-269-4	£9.99
Basildon Living Memories (pb)	1-85937-515-4	£9.99	Dorset Coast (pb)	1-85937-299-6	£9.99
Bath (pb)	1-85937-419-0	£9.99	Dorset Living Memories (pb)	1-85937-584-7	£9.99
Bedford (pb)	1-85937-205-8	£9.99	Down the Severn (pb)	1-85937-560-x	£9.99
Bedfordshire Living Memories	1-85937-513-8	£14.99	Down The Thames (pb)	1-85937-278-3	£9.99
Belfast (pb)	1-85937-303-8	£9.99	Down the Trent	1-85937-311-9	£14.99
Berkshire (pb)	1-85937-191-4	£9.99	East Anglia (pb)	1-85937-265-1	£9.99
Berkshire Churches	1-85937-170-1	£17.99	East Grinstead (pb)	1-85937-138-8	£9.99
Berkshire Living Memories	1-85937-332-1	£14.99	East London	1-85937-080-2	£14.99
Black Country	1-85937-497-2	£12.99	East Sussex (pb)	1-85937-606-1	£9.99
Blackpool (pb)	1-85937-393-3	£9.99	Eastbourne (pb)	1-85937-399-2	£9.99
Bognor Regis (pb)	1-85937-431-x	£9.99	Edinburgh (pb)	1-85937-193-0	£8.99
Bournemouth (pb)	1-85937-545-6	£9.99	England In The 1880s	1-85937-331-3	£17.99
Bradford (pb)	1-85937-204-x	£9.99	Essex - Second Selection	1-85937-456-5	£14.99
Bridgend (pb)	1-85937-386-0	£7.99	Essex (pb)	1-85937-270-8	£9.99
Bridgwater (pb)	1-85937-305-4	£9.99	Essex Coast	1-85937-342-9	£14.99
Bridport (pb)	1-85937-327-5	£9.99	Essex Living Memories	1-85937-490-5	£14.99
Brighton (pb)	1-85937-192-2	£8.99	Exeter	1-85937-539-1	£9.99
Bristol (pb)	1-85937-264-3	£9.99	Exmoor (pb)	1-85937-608-8	£9.99
British Life A Century Ago (pb)	1-85937-213-9	£9.99	Falmouth (pb)	1-85937-594-4	£9.99
Buckinghamshire (pb)	1-85937-200-7	£9.99	Folkestone (pb)	1-85937-124-8	£9.99
Camberley (pb)	1-85937-222-8	£9.99	Frome (pb)	1-85937-317-8	£9.99
Cambridge (pb)	1-85937-422-0	£9.99	Glamorgan	1-85937-488-3	£14.99
Cambridgeshire (pb)	1-85937-420-4	£9.99	Glasgow (pb)	1-85937-190-6	£9.99
Cambridgeshire Villages	1-85937-523-5	£14.99	Glastonbury (pb)	1-85937-338-0	£7.99
Canals And Waterways (pb)	1-85937-291-0	£9.99	Gloucester (pb)	1-85937-232-5	£9.99
Canterbury Cathedral (pb)	1-85937-179-5	£9.99	Gloucestershire (pb)	1-85937-561-8	£9.99
Cardiff (pb)	1-85937-093-4	£9.99	Great Yarmouth (pb)	1-85937-426-3	£9.99
Carmarthenshire (pb)	1-85937-604-5	£9.99	Greater Manchester (pb)	1-85937-266-x	£9.99
Chelmsford (pb)	1-85937-310-0	£9.99	Guildford (pb)	1-85937-410-7	£9.99
Cheltenham (pb)	1-85937-095-0	£9.99	Hampshire (pb)	1-85937-279-1	£9.99
Cheshire (pb)	1-85937-271-6	£9.99	Harrogate (pb)	1-85937-423-9	£9.99
Chester (pb)	1-85937-382 8	£9.99	Hastings and Bexhill (pb)	1-85937-131-0	£9.99
Chesterfield (pb)	1-85937-378-x	£9.99	Heart of Lancashire (pb)	1-85937-197-3	£9.99
Chichester (pb)	1-85937-228-7	£9.99	Helston (pb)	1-85937-214-7	£9.99
Churches of East Cornwall (pb)	1-85937-249-x	£9.99	Hereford (pb)	1-85937-175-2	£9.99
Churches of Hampshire (pb)	1-85937-207-4	£9.99	Herefordshire (pb)	1-85937-567-7	£9.99
Cinque Ports & Two Ancient Towns	1-85937-492-1	£14.99	Herefordshire Living Memories	1-85937-514-6	£14.99
Colchester (pb)	1-85937-188-4	£8.99	Hertfordshire (pb)	1-85937-247-3	£9.99
Cornwall (pb)	1-85937-229-5	£9.99	Horsham (pb)	1-85937-432-8	£9.99
Cornwall Living Memories	1-85937-248-1	£14.99	Humberside (pb)	1-85937-605-3	£9.99
Cotswolds (pb)	1-85937-230-9	£9.99	Hythe, Romney Marsh, Ashford (pb)	1-85937-256-2	£9.99
Cotswolds Living Memories	1-85937-255-4	£14.99	Ipswich (pb)	1-85937-424-7	£9.99
County Durham (pb)	1-85937-398-4	£9.99	Isle of Man (pb)	1-85937-268-6	£9.99
Croydon Living Memories (pb)	1-85937-162-0	£9.99	Isle of Wight (pb)	1-85937-429-8	£9.99
Cumbria (pb)	1-85937-621-5	£9.99	Isle of Wight Living Memories	1-85937-304-6	£14.99
Derby (pb)	1-85937-367-4	£9.99	Kent (pb)	1-85937-189-2	£9.99
Derbyshire (pb)	1-85937-196-5	£9.99	Kent Living Memories(pb)	1-85937-401-8	£9.99
Derbyshire Living Memories	1-85937-330-5	£14.99	Kings Lynn (pb)	1-85937-334-8	£9.99

Available from your local bookshop or from the publisher

Frith Book Co Titles (continued)

Lake District (pb)	1-85937-275-9	£9.99	Sherborne (pb)	1-85937-301-1	£9.99
Lancashire Living Memories	1-85937-335-6	£14.99	Shrewsbury (pb)	1-85937-325-9	£9.99
Lancaster, Morecambe, Heysham (pb)	1-85937-233-3	£9.99	Shropshire (pb)	1-85937-326-7	£9.99
Leeds (pb)	1-85937-202-3	£9.99	Shropshire Living Memories	1-85937-643-6	£14.99
Leicester (pb)	1-85937-381-x	£9.99	Somerset	1-85937-153-1	£14.99
Leicestershire & Rutland Living Memories	1-85937-500-6	£12.99	South Devon Coast	1-85937-107-8	£14.99
Leicestershire (pb)	1-85937-185-x	£9.99	South Devon Living Memories (pb)	1-85937-609-6	£9.99
Lighthouses	1-85937-257-0	£9.99	South East London (pb)	1-85937-263-5	£9.99
Lincoln (pb)	1-85937-380-1	£9.99	South Somerset	1-85937-318-6	£14.99
Lincolnshire (pb)	1-85937-433-6	£9.99	South Wales	1-85937-519-7	£14.99
Liverpool and Merseyside (pb)	1-85937-234-1	£9.99	Southampton (pb)	1-85937-427-1	£9.99
London (pb)	1-85937-183-3	£9.99	Southend (pb)	1-85937-313-5	£9.99
London Living Memories	1-85937-454-9	£14.99	Southport (pb)	1-85937-425-5	£9.99
Ludlow (pb)	1-85937-176-0	£9.99	St Albans (pb)	1-85937-341-0	£9.99
Luton (pb)	1-85937-235-x	£9.99	St Ives (pb)	1-85937-415-8	£9.99
Maidenhead (pb)	1-85937-339-9	£9.99	Stafford Living Memories (pb)	1-85937-503-0	£9.99
Maidstone (pb)	1-85937-391-7	£9.99	Staffordshire (pb)	1-85937-308-9	£9.99
Manchester (pb)	1-85937-198-1	£9.99	Stourbridge (pb)	1-85937-530-8	£9.99
Marlborough (pb)	1-85937-336-4	£9.99	Stratford upon Avon (pb)	1-85937-388-7	£9.99
Middlesex	1-85937-158-2	£14.99	Suffolk (pb)	1-85937-221-x	£9.99
Monmouthshire	1-85937-532-4	£14.99	Suffolk Coast (pb)	1-85937-610-x	£9.99
New Forest (pb)	1-85937-390-9	£9.99	Surrey (pb)	1-85937-240-6	£9.99
Newark (pb)	1-85937-366-6	£9.99	Surrey Living Memories	1-85937-328-3	£14.99
Newport, Wales (pb)	1-85937-258-9	£9.99	Sussex (pb)	1-85937-184-1	£9.99
Newquay (pb)	1-85937-421-2	£9.99	Sutton (pb)	1-85937-337-2	£9.99
Norfolk (pb)	1-85937-195-7	£9.99	Swansea (pb)	1-85937-167-1	£9.99
Norfolk Broads	1-85937-486-7	£14.99	Taunton (pb)	1-85937-314-3	£9.99
Norfolk Living Memories (pb)	1-85937-402-6	£9.99	Tees Valley & Cleveland (pb)	1-85937-623-1	£9.99
North Buckinghamshire	1-85937-626-6	£14.99	Teignmouth (pb)	1-85937-370-4	£7.99
North Devon Living Memories	1-85937-261-9	£14.99	Thanet (pb)	1-85937-116-7	£9.99
North Hertfordshire	1-85937-547-2	£14.99	Tiverton (pb)	1-85937-178-7	£9.99
North London (pb)	1-85937-403-4	£9.99	Torbay (pb)	1-85937-597-9	£9.99
North Somerset	1-85937-302-x	£14.99	Truro (pb)	1-85937-598-7	£9.99
North Wales (pb)	1-85937-298-8	£9.99	Victorian & Edwardian Dorset	1-85937-254-6	£14.99
North Yorkshire (pb)	1-85937-236-8	£9.99	Victorian & Edwardian Kent (pb)	1-85937-624-X	£9.99
Northamptonshire Living Memories	1-85937-529-4	£14.99	Victorian & Edwardian Maritime Album (pb)	1-85937-622-3	£9.99
Northamptonshire	1-85937-150-7	£14.99	Victorian and Edwardian Sussex (pb)	1-85937-625-8	£9.99
Northumberland Tyne & Wear (pb)	1-85937-281-3	£9.99	Villages of Devon (pb)	1-85937-293-7	£9.99
Northumberland	1-85937-522-7	£14.99	Villages of Kent (pb)	1-85937-294-5	£9.99
Norwich (pb)	1-85937-194-9	£8.99	Villages of Sussex (pb)	1-85937-295-3	£9.99
Nottingham (pb)	1-85937-324-0	£9.99	Warrington (pb)	1-85937-507-3	£9.99
Nottinghamshire (pb)	1-85937-187-6	£9.99	Warwick (pb)	1-85937-518-9	£9.99
Oxford (pb)	1-85937-411-5	£9.99	Warwickshire (pb)	1-85937-203-1	£9.99
Oxfordshire (pb)	1-85937-430-1	£9.99	Welsh Castles (pb)	1-85937-322-4	£9.99
Oxfordshire Living Memories	1-85937-525-1	£14.99	West Midlands (pb)	1-85937-209-9	£9.99
Paignton (pb)	1-85937-374-7	£7.99	West Sussex (pb)	1-85937-607-x	£9.99
Peak District (pb)	1-85937-280-5	£9.99	West Yorkshire (pb)	1-85937-201-5	£9.99
Pembrokeshire	1-85937-262-7	£14.99	Weston Super Mare (pb)	1-85937-306-2	£9.99
Penzance (pb)	1-85937-595-2	£9.99	Weymouth (pb)	1-85937-209-0	£9.99
Peterborough (pb)	1-85937-219-8	£9.99	Wiltshire (pb)	1-85937-277-5	£9.99
Picturesque Harbours	1-85937-208-2	£14.99	Wiltshire Churches (pb)	1-85937-171-x	£9.99
Piers	1-85937-237-6	£17.99	Wiltshire Living Memories (pb)	1-85937-396-8	£9.99
Plymouth (pb)	1-85937-389-5	£9.99	Winchester (pb)	1-85937-428-x	£9.99
Poole & Sandbanks (pb)	1-85937-251-1	£9.99	Windsor (pb)	1-85937-333-x	£9.99
Preston (pb)	1-85937-212-0	£9.99	Wokingham & Bracknell (pb)	1-85937-329-1	£9.99
Reading (pb)	1-85937-238-4	£9.99	Woodbridge (pb)	1-85937-498-0	£9.99
Redhill to Reigate (pb)	1-85937-596-0	£9.99	Worcester (pb)	1-85937-165-5	£9.99
Ringwood (pb)	1-85937-384-4	£7.99	Worcestershire Living Memories	1-85937-489-1	£14.99
Romford (pb)	1-85937-319-4	£9.99	Worcestershire	1-85937-152-3	£14.99
Royal Tunbridge Wells (pb)	1-85937-504-9	£9.99	York (pb)	1-85937-199-x	£9.99
Salisbury (pb)	1-85937-239-2	£9.99	Yorkshire (pb)	1-85937-186-8	£9.99
Scarborough (pb)	1-85937-379-8	£9.99	Yorkshire Coastal Memories	1-85937-506-5	£14.99
Sevenoaks and Tonbridge (pb)	1-85937-392-5	£9.99	Yorkshire Dales	1-85937-502-2	£14.99
Sheffield & South Yorks (pb)	1-85937-267-8	£9.99	Yorkshire Living Memories (pb)	1-85937-397-6	£9.99

See Frith books on the internet at www.francisfrith.co.uk

Frith Products & Services

Francis Frith would doubtless be pleased to know that the pioneering publishing venture he started in 1860 still continues today. Over a hundred and forty years later, The Francis Frith Collection continues in the same innovative tradition and is now one of the foremost publishers of vintage photographs in the world. Some of the current activities include:

Interior Decoration

Today Frith's photographs can be seen framed and as giant wall murals in thousands of pubs, restaurants, hotels, banks, retail stores and other public buildings throughout the country. In every case they enhance the unique local atmosphere of the places they depict and provide reminders of gentler days in an increasingly busy and frenetic world.

Product Promotions

Frith products are used by many major companies to promote the sales of their own products or to reinforce their own history and heritage. Frith promotions have been used by Hovis bread, Courage beers, Scots Porage Oats, Colman's mustard, Cadbury's foods, Mellow Birds coffee, Dunhill pipe tobacco, Guinness, and Bulmer's Cider.

Genealogy and Family History

As the interest in family history and roots grows world-wide, more and more people are turning to Frith's photographs of Great Britain for images of the towns, villages and streets where their ancestors lived; and, of course, photographs of the churches and chapels where their ancestors were christened, married and buried are an essential part of every genealogy tree and family album.

Frith Products

All Frith photographs are available Framed or just as Mounted Prints and Posters (size 23 x 16 inches). These may be ordered from the address below. From time to time other products - Address Books, Calendars, Table Mats, etc - are available.

The Internet

Already fifty thousand Frith photographs can be viewed and purchased on the internet through the Frith websites and a myriad of partner sites.

For more detailed information on Frith companies and products, look at these sites:

www.francisfrith.co.uk
www.francisfrith.com
(for North American visitors)

See the complete list of Frith Books at:

www.francisfrith.co.uk

This web site is regularly updated with the latest list of publications from the Frith Book Company. If you wish to buy books relating to another part of the country that your local bookshop does not stock, you may purchase on-line.

For further information, trade, or author enquiries please contact us at the address below:
The Francis Frith Collection, Frith's Barn, Teffont, Salisbury, Wiltshire, England SP3 5QP.
Tel: +44 (0)1722 716 376 Fax: +44 (0)1722 716 881 Email: sales@francisfrith.co.uk

See Frith books on the internet at www.francisfrith.co.uk

HOW TO ORDER YOUR FREE MOUNTED PRINT
and other Frith prints at half price

Mounted Print
Overall size 14 x 11 inches

Fill in and cut out this voucher and return it with your remittance for £2.25 (to cover postage and handling to UK addresses). For overseas addresses please include £4.00 post and handling.
Choose any photograph included in this book. Your SEPIA print will be A4 in size. It will be mounted in a cream mount with a burgundy rule line (overall size 14 x 11 inches).

Order additional Mounted Prints at HALF PRICE (only £7.49 each*)

If you would like to order more Frith prints from this book, possibly as gifts for friends and family, you can buy them at half price (with no additional postage and handling costs).

Have your Mounted Prints framed

For an extra £14.95 per print* you can have your mounted print(s) framed in an elegant polished wood and gilt moulding, overall size 16 x 13 inches (no additional postage and handling required).

---

* IMPORTANT!

These special prices are only available if you order at the same time as you order your free mounted print. You must use the ORIGINAL VOUCHER on this page (no copies permitted). We can only despatch to one address.

Voucher *for* **FREE** *and Reduced Price Frith Prints*

Please do not photocopy this voucher. Only the original is valid, so please fill it in, cut it out and return it to us with your order.

Picture ref no	Page number	Qty	Mounted @ £7.49	Framed + £14.95	Total Cost
		1	Free of charge*	£	£
			£7.49	£	£
			£7.49	£	£
			£7.49	£	£
			£7.49	£	£
			£7.49	£	£

Please allow 28 days for delivery

* Post & handling (UK) £2.25

Total Order Cost £

Title of this book . . . .

I enclose a cheque/postal order for £ . . . .
made payable to 'The Francis Frith Collection'

OR please debit my Mastercard / Visa / Switch / Amex card
(credit cards please on all overseas orders), details below

Card Number

Issue No (Switch only)   Valid from (Amex/Switch)

Expires   Signature

Name Mr/Mrs/Ms ....

Address ....

....

....

.... Postcode ....

Daytime Tel No ....

Email ....

Valid to 31/12/05

Send completed Voucher form to:
The Francis Frith Collection, Frith's Barn, Teffont, Salisbury, Wiltshire SP3 5QP

Would you like to find out more about Francis Frith?

We have recently recruited some entertaining speakers who are happy to visit local groups, clubs and societies to give an illustrated talk documenting Frith's travels and photographs. If you are a member of such a group and are interested in hosting a presentation, we would love to hear from you.

Our speakers bring with them a small selection of our local town and county books, together with sample prints. They are happy to take orders. A small proportion of the order value is donated to the group who have hosted the presentation. The talks are therefore an excellent way of fundraising for small groups and societies.

Can you help us with information about any of the Frith photographs in this book?

We are gradually compiling an historical record for each of the photographs in the Frith archive. It is always fascinating to find out the names of the people shown in the pictures, as well as insights into the shops, buildings and other features depicted.

If you recognize anyone in the photographs in this book, or if you have information not already included in the author's caption, do let us know. We would love to hear from you, and will try to publish it in future books or articles.

Our production team

Frith books are produced by a small dedicated team at offices in the converted Grade II listed 18th-century barn at Teffont near Salisbury, illustrated above. Most have worked with the Frith Collection for many years. All have in common one quality: they have a passion for the Frith Collection. The team is constantly expanding, but currently includes:

Jason Buck, John Buck, Douglas Mitchell-Burns, Ruth Butler, Heather Crisp, Isobel Hall, Maureen Harrison, Julian Hight, Peter Horne, James Kinnear, Karen Kinnear, Tina Leary, David Marsh, Sue Molloy, Kate Rotondetto, Dean Scource, Eliza Sackett, Terence Sackett, Sandra Sampson, Adrian Sanders, Sandra Sanger, Julia Skinner, Lewis Taylor, Shelley Tolcher, and Lorraine Tuck.